哎吔!
AIEEYAAA!

LEARN CHINESE THE *HARD* WAY

FROM ĀI TO ZÌ

BY

方南理
LARRY FEIGN

INESE
BY
G-FEIGN

D1472283

for Cathy

Third edition

Top Floor Books
imprint of stvdio media
PO Box 29
Silvermine Bay, Hong Kong
topfloorbooks.com

ISBN 978 962 7866 20 6

LEARNING CHINESE
IS EASY!

And if you believe that, you probably also believe in the Easter Bunny and that pigs can fly. If you're like most people in the process of learning Chinese, then the adjective to describe what you're going through is more likely unrepeatable in polite company. If you're just starting out, well, prepare for a rough ride.

Countless textbooks, audio/video lessons, and websites proclaim their methods to be *easy, easier, simple, instant.* Many are quite good, great even, but *easy?* Sorry to pop your bubble, but such promises only set you up for disappointment, discouragement, and devastation to your self-esteem.

But a hundred million Chinese four-year-olds speak perfect Chinese!

What choice do they have? If you were stuck day and night with people speaking nothing but Chinese, being sent to bed without sweet bean dessert if you didn't respond, then you'd be happily fluent right now. Total immersion learning absolutely works. But for those of us neither adopted by Chinese parents nor trapped in a remote Hunan village, prepare for the following booby traps as you advance across the linguistic minefields.

Mandarin vs. Cantonese, Shanghainese and a squillion other dialects

Mandarin, the national language, goes by so many names— *Zhōngwén, Pǔtōnghuà, Hànyǔ, Guóyǔ*—that Lesson One should be, "What do you even call it?" You should learn it if you're going to mainland China or Taiwan to study or do business. But unless you live in Beijing, don't expect to necessarily be able to eavesdrop on party conversations. For that, you'll also need Shanghainese in Shanghai, *minyu* in Fujian and Hainan, Taiwanese in Taiwan, and so on, not to mention Tibetan, Mongolian, Uygur, and other languages which dominate enormous swaths of the Motherland.

Cantonese sometimes feels like it was designed by a committee for the sole purpose of being impossible for foreigners to learn. However, if you live in Hong Kong, where Cantonese is the official dialect, then studying Mandarin would be like living in Paris yet learning Spanish just because it's the more widely-spoken Latin-based language. If you live outside China, and are seeking friendship or business in your nearest Chinatown, take into account that historically most Chinese emigrants came from southern China, and you'll get better service in Chinatown noodle shops by showing off your Cantonese or Hokkien. If it's movies you're into, remember that Bruce Lee, Jet Li, Chow Yun-fat, Tony Leung, Maggie Cheung and other stars you've heard of, are Hong Kongers who speak Cantonese in the majority of their films not meant for export (hence the ones which earn you hipster points).

It's incorrect to even label Mandarin and Cantonese as different dialects of a macro language called "Chinese". They may be rooted in some ancient Ur-Chinese and share similar writing systems, but they're as mutually incomprehensible to each other as Romanian and French, both Latin-based languages. *Yi* means *one* in Mandarin, while *yi* in Cantonese means *two*. It gets more complicated from there. So choose your Chinese lingo carefully.

Aside from being the "official" language, Mandarin's primary advantage over the rest is its tones.

Tones

Mandarin has four tones—or five, if you count the "neutral" tone. That doesn't mean you can somehow slur or fudge your tones and get away with it. You could end up losing an eye (眼睛 *yǎn jīng*) rather than just your eyeglasses (眼镜 *yǎn jìng*).

Still think you might get away with a little mistake in tone here and there? Try reciting the famous poem, *Shī Shì shí shī shǐ* (施氏食獅史), "The Lion-eating Poet in the Stone Den" by Chao Yuen Ren (趙元任):

> 石室詩士施氏，嗜獅，誓食十獅。
> 氏時時適市視獅。
> 十時，適十獅適市。
> 是時，適施氏適市。
> 氏視是十獅，恃矢勢，使是十獅逝世。
> 氏拾是十獅屍，適石室。
> 石室濕，氏使侍拭石室。
> 石室拭，氏始試食是十獅。
> 食時，始識是十獅屍，實十石獅屍。
> 試釋是事。

> *Shí shì shī shì Shī Shì, shì shī, shì shí shí shī.*
> *Shì shí shí shì shì shì shī.*
> *Shí shí, shì shí shī shì shì.*
> *Shì shí, shì Shī Shì shì shì.*
> *Shì shì shì shí shī, shì shǐ shì, shǐ shì shí shī shì shì.*
> *Shì shí shì shí shī shī, shì shí shì.*
> *Shí shì shī, Shì shǐ shì shì shí shì.*
> *Shí shì shì, Shì shǐ shì shí shì shí shī.*
> *Shí shí, shǐ shí shì shí shī shī, shí shí shí shī shī.*
> *Shì shì shì shì.*

A poet goes to market, kills ten lions with arrows, then drags them back to his den and eats them, *as long as the speaker gets the tones correct*. A single slip of tone can be lethal, resulting in a lion eating ten poets instead.

Poets are in greater danger in Cantonese. The general wisdom is that there are six major tones, and three sub-tones, for a total of nine, though others claim a fourth sub-tone, adding up to ten. Infuriatingly, most systems note only the six main tones, leaving you to guess whether "1" refers to "high level", "high falling", or "high clipped". If you make the logical conclusion that you can therefore get away with slight variances and still be understood, three minutes of conversation with a Cantonese native speaker will have you pulling the tongue from your head.

Chinese ears, by necessity, are so acutely attuned to the slightest subtleties of phonetics and pitch that their ears leave little margin for error. Which is outrageously unfair, if you think about it. Most English speakers, for example, have a reasonable tolerance for mispronunciation. When the pretty Chinese weather girls on Hong Kong English television report the day's *relative humility*, we know they're talking about moist air, not about government officials' shameless *elegance*—that is, *arrogance*.

Yet make a tiny error like I did, instructing a contractor in Cantonese to separate two rooms with a long wall—長牆 *cheung⁴ cheung⁴* (both fourth tone)—ending up instead with an enormous new picture window—窗 *cheung¹* (first tone). True story! To make matters more confusing, my contractor, from the island of 長洲 Cheung⁴ Chau¹, was surnamed 張 Cheung¹.

Writing

At first glance, reading and writing Chinese seems an insurmountable task. To be considered minimally literate, you need to know 3000 to 5000 different characters. How can there possibly be space inside a single human brain to fit all those spoken tones and written characters, and still have enough synapses left over to remember how to tie one's shoe?

Once you calm down from your panic, you begin to realize that there is a certain sense, even superiority, to the Chinese writing system. It's all based on pictures, assembled like little puzzles to make meaning.

For example, 日 is a picture of the sun (the line through the middle was originally a dot in the center), while you can't deny that 月 somewhat looks like an abstract crescent moon. Easy to remember! Squeeze them together into a single character and you get 明, which means "bright" or "clear"—in both a literal and a figurative sense. You don't even have to know how to say it in order to understand.

Sometimes combining the constituent parts, or radicals, produces a more metaphorical meaning. For example, take *woman* 女, which is clearly a picture of a female body modeling a string bikini, and *child* 子, which looks like a big whining mouth and two stubby waving arms. Long ago, some scholar decided, in an ancient Chinese Hallmark moment, that woman and child together—好— is the embodiment of *good*.

Feel better yet? Take a guess how to write "home" and "family".

A man, woman and child together? No such character. A housewife under a roof: 安? In fact, that word means "peace", presumably because her husband is out of the house. How about a pig 豕 under a roof 宀 to make 家? Seems like that should be the word for "pigsty", but no: that is indeed how you write "home" or "family". My guess is that whichever scholar was assigned to come up with that character must have had teenage children, took one glance at their rooms, and...need I explain further?

And that's it. By simply assembling and breaking down the parts, you too can read or write any Chinese character. For example:

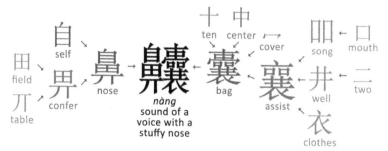

Self on a field over a table, singing over your clothes at the bottom of ten covered wells—齉—quite clearly means: the sound your voice makes when you have a stuffed nose. You knew that!

Simplified vs Traditional Characters

Of course, this handy method falls apart when you switch to simplified characters. Take 魚 "fish" for example. True to its meaning, the traditional character resembles a fishy head on top, scaled body in the middle, and four fins happily propelling it upriver. For the simplified 鱼 the fins were amputated, kind of an endorsement of the inhumane practice of harvesting shark fins.

Try "door" 門. Looks exactly like the swinging doors on Old West saloons and Hong Kong pawn shops. Until the Simplifiers tore off both panels, removing all hope of privacy: 门. They could have at least removed the hinge they left dangling in the top corner.

So, which Chinese do you learn? Mandarin or Cantonese? Traditional or simplified characters? By now you're thinking: *None of the above! I'm taking up Italian instead!*

CONVENTIONS USED IN THIS BOOK

Each English word is presented with Mandarin and Cantonese meanings. Often these are variants of each other, but sometimes the Mandarin and Cantonese terms are quite different.

Mandarin words are written in simplified characters, Cantonese in traditional characters.

Pronunciations are a different matter. For Mandarin this book employs *hanyu pinyin,* as used in mainland China, which might annoy Taiwan residents, who use a confusing mix of the anachronistic Wade-Giles system and two variants of pinyin. Let's stick with Mainland-style pinyin, which is refreshingly user-friendly.

MANDARIN – The four major tones:

1 – High (macron dash), as in *zhōng* 中 (China)
2 – Rising (rising accent), as in *wén* 文 (language)
3 – Falling-rising (breve mark), as in *hěn* 很 (very)
4 – Falling (falling accent), as in *guài* 怪 (bewildering)

Hence, the sentence, 中文很怪 *Zhōng wén hěn guài,* provides a pocket-sized reminder of the four tones.

Cantonese is more problematic. There is no "standard" Romanization, which leads to a lot of tongue-twisting confusion. Your Hong Kong phrase book may use the Yale system to advise you to visit 尖沙咀 *Jīm Sā Jéui*, while another follows Sidney Lau's system calling it *Jim¹ Sa¹ Jui²*, and a more academic dictionary employs the clumsy *jyutping* to direct you to *Zim¹ Saa¹ Zeoi²*, even though the Hong Kong government, and most maps, buses and trains cling to the Eitel/Dyer-Ball system in naming Hong Kong's main tourist district *Tsim Sha Tsui*. This book uses the Sidney Lau system, simply because it's the least intimidating among numerous imperfect choices.

CANTONESE – The six major tones:

1 – High falling, level, or clipped, as in *saam¹* 三 (three)
2 – Middle rising, as in *gau²* 九 (nine)
3 – Middle level or clipped, as in *baat³* 八 (eight)
4 – Low falling, as in *ling⁴* 零 (zero)
5 – Low rising, as in *leung⁵* 兩 (two)
6 – Low level or clipped, as in *sap⁶* 十 (ten)

So logical and easy!

DISCLAIMER

And now, after all that: a confession.

This book is neither a dictionary nor a phrase book. In fact, I don't expect you to learn a thing from it. If it appears to you like just a random assortment of words with gags attached, that's pretty much how it came about.

On the other hand, that's exactly how toddlers acquire their first language: grabbing words and phrases as they fall from the air. And it's more or less how I learned Cantonese—by roaming Hong Kong streets and engaging in random conversations based on whatever encounters I happened to have. My original repertoire of Chinese characters came from studying advertisements on trains and buses and flipping through hefty dictionaries to discover their meanings (now made easier with smartphone dictionaries), which meant that for years my reading ability was biased toward promotional hyperbole. By contrast, I studied Mandarin with formal tutoring and textbooks, so I probably have a better literal grasp of Mandarin grammar. But Cantonese feels more natural to me, because I learned it the way a child would.

So please treat this book as a collection of linguistic snapshots of China and Hong Kong, the way you might an illustrated travel or recipe book: none can tell you the full story of a place, but perhaps you'll come away with a few impressions of this strange and wonderful hyperactive mass of humanity, and a few words with which to express them.

HOW TO USE THIS BOOK

MANDARIN
Simplified characters
+ pinyin

CANTONESE
Traditional characters
+ Lau pronunciation

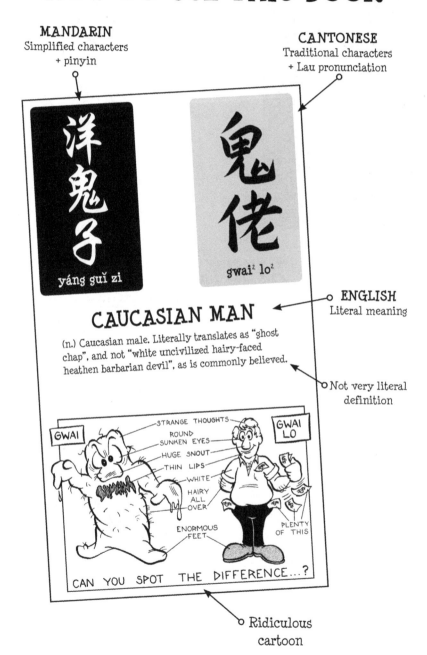

yáng guǐ zi

gwai² lo²

ENGLISH
Literal meaning

CAUCASIAN MAN

(n.) Caucasian male. Literally translates as "ghost chap", and not "white uncivilized hairy-faced heathen barbarian devil", as is commonly believed.

Not very literal
definition

GWAI

GWAI LO

STRANGE THOUGHTS

ROUND
SUNKEN EYES

HUGE SNOUT

THIN LIPS

WHITE

HAIRY
ALL
OVER

ENORMOUS
FEET

PLENTY
OF THIS

CAN YOU SPOT THE DIFFERENCE...?

Ridiculous
cartoon

āi yā

ai¹ ya¹

AIEEYAAA!

(excl.) Expresses delight, dismay, joy, pain, love, hate...or anything you want it to mean. The foreigner who pronounces this with precision will gain new respect from Chinese colleagues, especially when uttered every few seconds, anytime, anywhere, for any reason.

zhēn jiǔ

jam¹ gau³

ACUPUNCTURE

(n.) Treatment involving needles stuck
all over your body; typically painless...
until you get stuck with the bill.

gǔ dǒng

gwoo² dung²

ANTIQUE

(n.) Cheap ornaments which miraculously age a thousand years between the factory and the street markets.

guāng tóu

gwong¹ tau⁴

BALD

(adj.) Sign of prosperity in China.
Think of it not as losing hair,
but gaining face.

13

zhú

juk[1]

BAMBOO

(n.) Used for scaffolding on tall buildings; also used for food. Hopefully not at the same time.

yín háng

ngan⁴ hong⁴

BANK

(n.) Temple of worship to the indigenous religion of Greater China.

AND ON YOUR RIGHT IS HONG KONG'S GRAND HOLY TEMPLE.

dà dǎn   daai⁶ daam²

BIG BLADDER

(n.) The Chinese equivalent of "a lot of guts";
though in either language it's a mystery why
courage is associated with a swollen urinary
or digestive tract.

shū

sue[1]

BOOK

(n.) Considered bad luck by gamblers, since it sounds like 输(輸): to lose. Which is why the only books most people have anything to do with are their bank book and their book-ie.

YOU'RE READING A **BOOK**?! BUT I THOUGHT THAT WAS BAD LUCK!

NOT THIS ONE!

THE BIBLE? DO YOU THINK GOD IS GOING TO HELP YOU WIN AT GAMBLING?

WHY NOT? IT TELLS RIGHT HERE ABOUT TURNING 2 INTO 5000!

OH? WHICH SCRIPTURE IS THAT?

MARK 6! *

I SHOULD HAVE KNOWN!

* Mark 6:38-44

shuā yá

chaat³ nga⁴

BRUSH TEETH

(v.) Chinese do it before breakfast.
Westerners do it after. Further proof of
that East and West shall never meet.

mǎi

maai[5]

BUY

(v.) With only a slight shift in tone, sounds just like 卖(賣) *mài (maai⁵)* : to sell.
Never mind if you get the tone wrong; either way you'll make a profit.

jīn

gan[1]

CATTY

(n.) Catty. Chinese unit of weight
roughly equal to 1.3 pounds or 600 grams.
Unless, of course, you're a foreigner.

yáng guǐ zi

gwai² lo²

CAUCASIAN MAN

(n.) Caucasian male. Literally translates as "ghost chap", and not "white uncivilized hairy-faced heathen barbarian devil", as is commonly believed.

GWAI

GWAI LO

STRANGE THOUGHTS
ROUND SUNKEN EYES
HUGE SNOUT
THIN LIPS
WHITE
HAIRY ALL OVER
ENORMOUS FEET
PLENTY OF THIS

CAN YOU SPOT THE DIFFERENCE...?

guǐ pó

gwai² po⁴

CAUCASIAN WOMAN

(n.) Caucasian female; literally "ghost granny".
A sadly apt term, since white women in China
stand a ghost of a chance of any man, western
or Asian, asking them out.

zhōng wén

jung¹ man⁴

CHINESE LANGUAGE

(n.) Literally means "language of
the nation around which the rest of
the world revolves." And you always
thought that was English!

kuài zi

faai³ ji²

CHOPSTICKS

(n.) Chopticks. The original digital
technology, controlled entirely by
one's digits (fingers).

shèng dàn jié

sing³ daan³ jit³

CHRISTMAS

(n.) Major holiday which, in China, falls in April, when final manufacturing orders for the shopping season come in.

SANTA, DO YOU REALLY MAKE ALL THOSE TOYS AT THE NORTH POLE?

OF COURSE, YOUNG LADY. HO! HO! HO!

THEN HOW COME LAST YEAR ALL MY TOYS SAID "MADE IN CHINA"?

HO! HO! HO! THEY ONLY SAY THAT. THEY'RE REALLY MADE BY ME AND MY TRUSTY ELVES. HO! HO! HO!

HO HO HO. FALSIFYING COUNTRY OF ORIGIN LABELS.

CUSTOMS DEPT.

gōng wù yuán

gung¹ mo⁶ yuen⁴

CIVIL SERVANT

(n.) A misnomer, considering they are typically far from civil and don't know the meaning of service.

清洁

qīng jié

清潔

ching¹ git³

CLEAN

(adj.) State of being when rubbish is transferred from your property to your neighbor's.

tóu sù

tau⁴ so³

COMPLAIN

(v.) Something few people do,
since even fewer people listen.

zàn shǎng

jaan³ seung²

COMPLIMENT

(v./n.) Westerners finds it rude when a compliment is rejected, while Chinese consider it arrogant when one is accepted. Insults, however, find common cultural ground.

mào pái

mo⁶ paai⁴

COUNTERFEIT

(adj.) Counterfeit. They say that imitation is the sincerest form of flattery. And anyone who thinks flattery is out of style has never been to China.

biǎo jie

biu² je²

COUSIN

(n.) Specifically means older female cousin other than the daughter of one's father's brothers. And if you can remember that, you're doing better than most Chinese!

SO, IF YOUR **YI MA'S**① HUSBAND'S **TONG DAAI LO'S**② WIFE'S **YI SAANG'S**③ **JAT JAI**④ IS MY HUSBAND'S **BIU SO'S**⑤ **SUK FOO**⑥, AND I'M A MONTH OLDER, THAT MAKES ME YOUR **TONG GA JE**⑦, RIGHT?

NO, STUPID! I'M NOT YOUR **SOH TONG SAI LO**⑧! ... I'M YOUR **BIU DAI**⑨, SO YOU'RE MY **BIU JE**!

LI FAMILY REUNION

1) 姨媽 Mother's elder sister
2) 堂大佬 Father's brother's son (older)
3) 姨甥 Sister's son
4) 姪仔 Brother's son
5) 表嫂 Mother's sister's son's wife (older)
6) 叔父 Father's younger brother
7) 堂家姐 Father's brother's daughter (older)
8) 疏堂細佬 Father's brother's son (younger)
9) 表弟 Mother's sister's son (younger)

guò mǎ lù

gwoh³ ma⁵ lo⁶

CROSS THE STREET

(v.) Cross the street. Greater China's
most popular daredevil sport.

yá yī

nga⁴ yi¹

DENTIST

(n.) Dentist. Someone who puts gold in your mouth and takes it out of your pocket.

huà

wa^6

DIALECT

(n.) Chinese isn't the only language with
mutually unintelligible dialects, though
it at least has a unified writing system.

DIE

(v.) Commonly used as a curse, though saying it too often can lead to a self-fulfilling prophecy.

 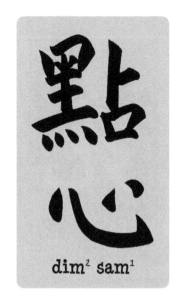

diǎn xīn

dim² sam¹

DIM SUM

(n.) Dim sum. Literally means "a little piece of heart"...
or liver or intestine or bladder, or whatever else can be
rolled up, steamed or fried.

lóng

lung[4]

1. DRAGON
2. QUEUE

(n.) Dragon. In Cantonese, also means queue, aptly enough, since both are mythical phenomena.

là yā

laap⁶ aap³

DRIED DUCK

(n.) Popular snack which seems more useful as table tennis paddles.

chī

sik⁶

EAT

(v.) A proverb says that "Chinese will eat anything whose back faces heaven." Which might explain why, at Chinese banquets, people kowtow with their fingers instead of bending down.

dàn

daan[6]

EGG

(n.) In China, even something as ordinary
as an egg is never quite that simple.

TWO EGGS, OVER EASY!

YES, SIR. WILL THOSE BE PIGEON, DUCK, QUAIL, CHICKEN, GOOSE, HUMMINGBIRD, PARTRIDGE, PELICAN, FLAMINGO, MONGOOSE, ALLIGATOR...

diàn tī

din⁶ tai¹

ELEVATOR / LIFT

(n.) Moving structure whose speed is in direct relation to the number of times you jab the up, down, or floor number buttons.

yīng wén

ying¹ man⁴

ENGLISH LANGUAGE

(n.) Once the living language of Shakespeare, now being bludgeoned to death by Asian t-shirt manufacturers.

kǎo shì

haau² si³

EXAMINATION

(n.) The be-all and end-all to life for Chinese students, or at least their parents.

miàn

min⁶

FACE

(n.) Everyone has one glued
to their skull, so why is it
so easy to lose?

yú

yue⁴

FISH

(n.) Creatures occasionally found among the other colorful contents of Asian waters.

I WANT TO MAKE SURE THEY FEEL AT HOME!

xiǎo jiǎo

jaat³ geuk³

FOOT BINDING

(n.) Archaic practice, which might be the only hope for foreigners shopping for shoes in China.

46

 wài guó rén

 ngoi⁶ gwok³ yan⁴

FOREIGNER

(n.) Denotes a white person living in a non-white country, as opposed to a non-white in a white country, who is "just another unwelcome Asian immigrant".

OUR NEW ACCOUNTS MANAGER ARRIVES FROM THE U.K. TOMORROW.

ANOTHER FOREIGNER? SHOULDN'T WE BE HIRING MORE LOCALS?

OF COURSE! FOR EVERY FOREIGNER HIRED, WE HIRE THREE LOCALS!

ASSISTANT MANAGERS?

NO, A DRIVER AND TWO MAIDS!

jiào zuò

giu³ jo⁶

FORENAME

(v.) Westerners enjoy laughing at the ludicrous English names many Chinese assign themselves; if only those foreigners knew how their own Chinese names sound to civilized ears.

chǎo yóu yú

chaau² yau⁴ yue⁴

1. FRIED CUTTLEFISH
2. TO BE FIRED

(n.) Slang for "given the sack." Which explains why this item is not found on the menus of company canteens.

péng yǒu

pang⁴ yau⁵

FRIEND

(n.) What others call you if you're rich or influential or can refer them some business; otherwise, they don't call you at all.

FRED, MEET MARIA. YOU TWO HAVE SO MUCH IN COMMON... YOU EACH MAKE *UNDER* US$50,000 A MONTH!

qīng wā

tin⁴ gai¹

FROG

(n.) Common delicacy in French and Chinese cuisine. Proof that neither are such picky eaters as they claim.

huā yuán

fa¹ yuen⁴

GARDEN

(n.) Deliberate misnomer applied to
colorless concrete housing estates
in Hong Kong and Shenzhen.

COW PASTURE

SHENZHEN

hǎo

ho²

GOOD / VERY / OKAY

(adj./adv.) Can also mean *fine, well, nice, likely.* Sprinkled liberally in every sentence, people will think your Chinese is *hao hao hao. Hao? Hao!*

zài jiàn

joi³ gin³

GOODBYE

(excl.) Farewell salutation used mainly by foreigners eager to impress each other. Chinese prefer the expression "Bah-byyyyyyyyyyeee!"

gǎng

gong²

HARBOR

(n.) The world-famous harbors of Hong Kong
and Shanghai have long provided safe harbor
to foreign ships and visitors, as well as
garbage and sewage from closer to home.

hāi

ha¹ lo¹

HELLO / HI

(excl.) What Chinese children say when trapped in elevators with foreigners or when goaded by parents to "practice their English" if a westerner is within hearing range.

liáng chá

leung⁴ cha⁴

HERBAL MEDICINE

(n.) Potions which cure any illness by tasting so incredibly vile that your body heals itself just to avoid being subjected to a further dose.

pá shān

pa⁴ saan¹

HIKE

(v./n.) The act of ascending to a higher elevation to reach a specific goal.

HIKING EUROPEAN STYLE

HIKING ASIAN STYLE

dǎ

da²

1. HIT
2. DOZEN

(v./n.) Words like this make you want to hit
whoever invented this language dozens of times!

sài mǎ

paau² ma⁵

HORSE RACE

(n.) The single legacy of colonialism that no Chinese has ever called a historical shame, especially not when #7, Golden Luck, is leading in the fourth.

yī yuàn

yi[1] yuen[6]

HOSPITAL

(n.) Place where you have to be
patient if you want to be a patient.

wǒ

ngoh[5]

I / ME

(pron.) The only person who exists
in a nation of 1.3 billion.

shēn fèn zhèng

san¹ fan⁶ jing³

IDENTITY CARD

(n.) Something the government requires you to carry under penalty of prosecution, knowing that most people would take one look at their photo and throw it away!

fǎ guān

faat³ gwoon¹

JUDGE

(n.) Man who wears a blonde wig, frilly dress, and pantyhose in public, and sends other men to prison for doing the same.

fān chuán

faan⁴ suen⁶

JUNK BOAT

(n.) Traditional sailing craft which once
dominated Asian seas and harbors; nowadays
dominating only misleading tourist brochures.

yá zi

sai³ lo⁶

KID

(n.) Diminutive creature utilized
to hold up traffic on sidewalks.

wěn

sek³

KISS

(v.) Implosive exchange of salivary fluids, often applied to children, karaoke lounge hostesses, and personal financial statements.

kē tóu

kau³ tau⁴

KOWTOW

(n./v.) The ancient custom of "striking the head" on the ground has been replaced by polite finger-tapping at the table, for very practical reasons.

tián hǎi

tin⁴ hoi²

LANDFILL /RECLAMATION

(n.) Government's method of converting the natural environment into natural profits for property developers.

lǜ shī

lut⁶ si¹

LAWYER

(n.) What hucksters and shysters do for a living when they're not clever enough to go into advertising.

xué

hok⁶

LEARN

(v.) The reason that foreigners find Chinese so hard to learn isn't because they're stupid or the language is difficult, but because no one will allow them to learn it!

shēng kōng

hing¹ gung¹

LEVITATE

(v.) The magical ability to fly, which all
Chinese people have, according to TV historical
dramas. So why don't more people use it to
beat the morning crowds on the train?

SUNG DYNASTY RUSH HOUR

tú shū guǎn

to⁴ sue¹ gwoon²

LIBRARY

(n.) Literally means "drawing book room",
a name taken too literally by too many
library book users.

chuī niú

che¹ daai⁶ paau³

1. LIE / BOAST
2. BLOW BULL / FIRE CANNON

(v.) The Chinese version of "shooting off at the mouth".

乱扔

luàn rēng

揼垃圾

dam² laap⁶ saap³

LITTER

(v.) If God had meant for us not to litter, he wouldn't have created drink cartons, Styrofoam lunch boxes, or horse race betting slips.

ài

oi³

LOVE

(n./v.) Dangerous condition associated with falling, madness, hypnotic states, and various heart disorders.

利是

lì shì

利是

lei[6] si[6]

LUCKY MONEY

(n.) Annual tariff levied by children and apartment building security guards.

ào mén

o³ moon⁴

MACAU

(n.) Former colony which boasts unique cuisine, Mediterranean architecture, and quaint Old World charm...but who goes there for that?

má jiàng

ma⁴ jeuk³

MAHJONG

(n.) Popular noise-making activity,
particularly since firecrackers were banned.

HOW TO PLAY MA JEUK (MAH JONG)

① DISTRIBUTE AMMUNITION

② ERECT FORTIFICATIONS

③ EXCHANGE MONEY

④ LET THE BATTLE BEGIN!

nǚ yōng

gung¹ yan⁴

MAID

(n.) Victims of poverty back home who
become victims of wealth in Hong Kong.

MARRIAGE

(n.) Union between a man and
the other woman in his life.

wǔ shù gwok³ sut⁶

MARTIAL ARTS

(n.) China's national sport...and you always
thought that was queue-jumping.

ròu

yuk[6]

MEAT

(n.) Chinese claim westerners eat too much of it; maybe they're afraid there won't be any left for them.

cài dān

choi³ paai⁴

MENU

(n.) List of food items, often indistinguishable
from the catalog of attractions at the local zoo.

zhōng qiū

baat³ yuet⁶ sap⁶ ng⁵

MID-AUTUMN FESTIVAL

(n.) Moon Festival (fifteenth day of the eighth
lunar month), and Cantonese euphemism for the
part of the body which most resembles the moon.

85

shǒu jī

sau² din⁶

MOBILE PHONE

(n.) Less a means of communication than
a means of preventing communication.

qián

chin[4]

MONEY

(n.) Of course it's more important than love. Over time, romantic interest wanes, but compound interest gains.

yuè liàng

yuet⁶ gwong¹

MOON

(n.) Scientists say it's a bleak, lifeless, airless environment. In that case, it must look a lot like the outskirts of Guangzhou.

yí dòng

yi⁴ dung⁶

MOVE

(v.) Physical impossibility for mountains, concrete buildings, and people who sit in the aisle seat on the bus.

gōng xǐ fā cái

gung¹ hei² faat³ choi⁴

NEW YEAR GREETING

(excl.) Literally means, "Congratulations, get rich," a condition attributable at this time of year exclusively to hair stylists.

bào zhǐ

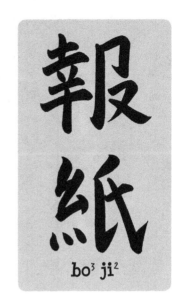

bo³ ji²

NEWSPAPER

(n.) These days few contain any actual news,
since no one reads them for that anyway.

zào yīn

cho³ yam¹

NOISE

(n.) There's a Chinese saying: "Where there's no noise there's no fun." In which case, Hong Kong must be the happiest city on the planet!

fèi huà

fong¹ maau⁶

NONSENSE

(n.) Any criticism leveled at this
extraordinary book.

bí zi

bei[6]

NOSE

(n.) Yet another thing which westerners have in gross excess, while Asians make do with more economical compact models.

AIYEEYAAA!! WILL YOU QUIT PUSHING?!!

QUEUE HERE
TICKET HOLDERS ONLY

SORRY. I DIDN'T REALIZE.

méi yǒu

mo⁵

NOT HAVE

(v.) Automatic conditioned response of salesclerks to any request which requires thought or movement.

wū lóng

woo[1] lung[4]

1. OOLONG TEA
2. FOOL

(n.) The former is not normally found in Hong Kong restaurants. The latter too often is.

lè guān zhě

lok[6] gwoon[1]

OPTIMIST

(n.) One who says that the future holds nothing but promise. A pessimist is one who says the same thing.

zàn tíng

jaam⁶ ting⁴

OUT OF SERVICE

(adj.) Sign so commonly seen on taxis,
that a "temporarily *in* service" sign
would make more sense.

zhǐ

ji²

PAPER

(n.) First invented in China 105 C.E.
First wrinkled up and tossed on the
ground 105¼ C.E.

jiè guò

je³ je³

PARDON ME

(excl.) Words mainly heard from newcomers to this part of the world, who should be pardoned for thinking anyone will heed such a request.

bǐ

bat[1]

PEN / PENCIL / BRUSH

(n.) Can mean any writing implement. No wonder so many foreigners give up after their first pen—*er*, brush—with Chinese!

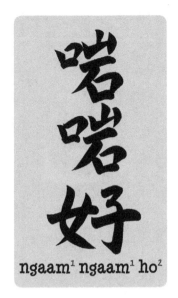

gāng gāng hǎo

ngaam¹ ngaam¹ ho²

PERFECT

(adj.) Optimistic terminology heard
most often in side street boutiques.

pāi zhào

ying² seung³

PHOTOGRAPH

(v.) Two-dimensional image composed
of light, color, contrast, and V-fingers.

hǎi dào

hoi² do⁶

PIRATE

(n.) Bandits who formerly used islands in the South China Sea as bases for rapine and plunder. These days they work from offices in Hong Kong and Shanghai.

sù liào dài

gaau¹ doi⁶

PLASTIC BAG

(n.) Marine organisms which inhabit coastal and inland waterways, sometimes seen stuffed with vegetables or designer clothing and carried on the street before being returned to the sea.

zhū ròu

jue¹ yuk⁶

PORK

(n.) Automatic additive to nearly every dish in nearly every restaurant throughout all of China.

jià qián

ga³ chin⁴

PRICE

(n.) Cost of a product or service; often dependent upon the country of origin... not of the item, but of the customer.

fā yīn

faat³ yam¹

PRONUNCIATION

(n.) A lost cause for foreigners. If, by sheer accident, you do get both the sounds and tones right, people will assume you were actually mispronouncing something else.

gǔ guài

gwaai³

QUEER

(n.) A man who is more interested
in women or men than in money.

pái duì

paai⁴ dui⁶

QUEUE

(v.) To wait in an orderly line without pushing,
shoving or cutting in place. Are you kidding?

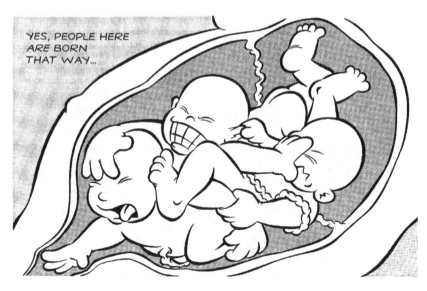

YES, PEOPLE HERE
ARE BORN
THAT WAY...

QUIET / SILENT

(adj.) Politicians always refer to the "silent majority". If only there were such a thing!

yǔ

yue⁵

RAIN

(n.) Acidic substance which, with a drop of oil,
might make a rather fine salad dressing.

fàng sōng

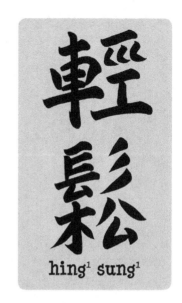

hing¹ sung¹

RELAX

(v.) Activity in which one engages in loud, overbearing, frenetic actions for the sake of making it impossible for others to relax.

yǒu qián

yau⁵ chin⁴

RICH

(adj.) State which leads to atrophy of the brain, heart and spine, whereby otherwise rational, intelligent people oppose genuine democracy for Hong Kong and China.

jié fěi

gip³ fei²

ROBBER

(n.) People who discover that the streets of new China aren't paved with gold and choose to steal it instead.

làng màn

long[6] maan[6]

ROMANTIC

(adj.) Situation or feeling associated with love and passion, though not necessarily for other people.

cū bào

cho¹ lo⁵

RUDE

(adj.) Everyone complains about rude behavior in China, but nobody does anything about it, because that would be ruder still!

yáo yán

yiu⁴ yin⁴

RUMOR

(n.) The difference between rumor and fact is that the latter is rarely taken seriously by Asian investors.

gōng zī

yan⁴ gung¹

SALARY

(n.) Also means "artificial", as in the division in pay scale and benefits between expatriate and local staff in many companies.

shòu huò yuán

sau⁶ foh³ yuen⁴

SALES CLERK

(n.) Someone who knows the words to all the latest K-Pop tunes and each intimate detail of the love lives of every local TV star, but can't tell you the difference between a vacuum cleaner and a coffee machine.

hǎi cǎo

hoi² cho²

SEAWEED

(n.) Slimy things found in the water, or at least some of them.

jǐng wèi

gwoon² lei⁵ yuen⁴

SECURITY GUARD

(n.) If you find a scrawny old man sleeping in your building's foyer, don't call the security guard. He *is* the security guard!

SERVICE

(n.) Quaint practice applicable only to customers with wheelie suitcases filled with money.

yú chì

yue⁴ chi³

SHARK FIN SOUP

(n.) The only health benefit of this nutritionless cartilege stew is to the health of the restaurant owner's bank balance.

SORRY, SIR — I THINK IT NOT COOKED LONG ENOUGH! MAYBE YOU TRY ANOTHER DISH, OK?

guàng jiē

maai[5] ye[5]

SHOP

(v.) Modern equivalent of hunting and gathering, though in present-day China it's mostly gathering.

WHAT SHALL WE PARTAKE OF THIS EVENING -- THE THEATRE, A SYMPHONY OR A GALLERY EXHIBITION?

WHAT WE SHOPPING FOR TONIGHT -- CLOTHES, FURNITURE OR DISHES?

LONDON

HONG KONG

lín yù

chung¹ leung⁴

SHOWER

(v.) Standing under falling water has opposite effects on Chinese and westerners; proof positive that they are in fact different species.

gē xīng

goh¹ sing¹

SINGING STAR

(n.) Mannekin with a nose job, filed teeth and expensive hair, whose Autotuned voice would set hearts throbbing if only the lip synching was in time to the synthesized track.

chòu dòu fu

chau³ dau⁶ foo⁶

SMELLY TOFU

(n.) Bean curd fermented in an extract of the unwashed socks of six football teams, then fried in oil that was rancid before your grandmother was born, yet actually tastes really, really good (try it).

shé gēng

se⁵ gang¹

SNAKE SOUP

(n.) Succulent serpent stew served in several savory specialties, such as cobra consomme, python puree, and viper vichyssoise.

shuō

sik¹ gong²

SPEAK

(v.) Foreigners in China are often accused of not bothering to speak a foreign language. That isn't true: many of them speak English!

tŭ

to³ taam⁴

SPIT

(v.) Sensible sanitary method for disposal of excess mucous, as opposed to the foreign habit of emptying it into a cloth and carrying it around in your pocket.

bài jiā zi

baai⁶ ga¹ jai²

SPOILED BRAT

(n.) Useless offspring of billionaires; the unsung heroes of Asian economies, for frittering away family funds locally, rather than letting Daddy squander it on mistresses across the border.

dú shū

duk[6] sue[1]

STUDY

(v.) The key to a brighter financial future,
though not necessarily through education.

sha gua

faan¹ sue⁴

STUPID IDIOT

(adj.) In Mandarin, call someone a melon;
in Cantonese, a sweet potato. Be sure of your
geography when you go vegetable shopping!

rì luò

yat⁶ lok⁶

SUNSET

(n.) Time of day when brilliant colors tint the smog, though mainly from neon lights rather than some mythical celestial body.

xìng

sing³

SURNAME

(v.) When someone tells you, "Sing Lo", he's telling you his family name, not his vocal range.

dǎ bāo

da² baau¹

TAKE-AWAY

(v./adj.) Also means "to bag a corpse".
Not a service you expect to find in
vegetarian restaurants.

chū zū chē

dik^1 si^6

TAXI

(n.) Vehicles which must have been designed by theoretical mathematicians, since they contain a device which produces imaginary numbers.

chá

cha[4]

TEA

(n.) In theory, the only thing English and Chinese have in common. But certainly not in practice.

diàn huà

din⁶ wa⁶

TELEPHONE

(n.) Primary weapon of mass
miscommunication by Hong
Kong secretaries.

shí fēn

sap⁶ fan¹

1. TEN MINUTES
2. COMPLETELY

(n./adv.) About how long it takes
most foreigners to *completely*
give up learning Chinese.

san

saam[1]

THREE

(n./adj.) Number of times you have to
ask before a Chinese person will tell you
what you suspected in the first place.

xiǎo fèi

tip³ si⁶

TIP

(n.) Small change left in appreciation...of
the threat to your safety if a tip isn't left!

yá

nga[4]

TOOTH / TEETH

(n.) Bright sparkly things featured in toothpaste ads and government press conferences.

kě jìn

jun⁶ leung⁶

TRY MY BEST

(v.) The ubiquitous response to any request, which actually means, "I'll do nothing of the sort."

săn

je¹

UMBRELLA

(n.) Device for the removal of eyeballs from anyone over five feet tall.

dà xué

daai⁶ hok⁶

UNIVERSITY

(n.) Institution once attended for the sake
of higher learning; nowadays attended for
the sake of higher earning.

shū cài

choi³

VEGETABLE

(n.) Chinese never overcook them
nor eat them raw, unlike westerners,
who eat them no other way.

jǐng

ging²

VIEW

(n.) Like everything else you get in
China, it doesn't last very long.

xǐng lái

hei² san¹

WAKE UP

(v.) What many people do between 6:00 and
7:00 a.m., and if they're in government,
again at 4:45 p.m.

shuǐ

sui²

WATER

(n.) Minor component of the substance that issues from your kitchen tap.

ARE YOU **SURE** THIS WATER IS TREATED??

tiān qì

tin¹ hei³

WEATHER

(n.) In mainland China, it's manipulated by the government, while in Hong Kong it's sponsored on TV by expensive Swiss watch brands, which is ironic, since watches are meant to be accurate.

hūn lǐ

fan¹ lai⁵

WEDDING

(n.) Whoever said you can't put a price on
love never planned a Chinese wedding.

chuāng zi

cheung[1]

WINDOW

(n.) Openings in buildings which allow
air in and garbage out.

shì jiè

sai³ gaai³

WORLD

(n.) Place somewhere beyond the Beijing suburbs where manufactured exports go and foreigners come from.

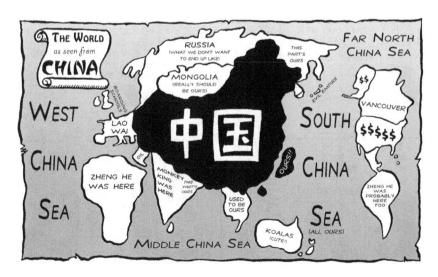

duì

hai⁶

YES

(excl.) A tiny word that causes major east-west misunderstanding. Whereas both westerners and Chinese will answer the question, "Isn't Chinese hopelessly difficult?" with "Yes," the westerner means, "Yes it is," while the Chinese means, "Yes, that's literally correct: it *isn't.*"

dòng wù yuán

dung⁶ mat⁶ yuen⁴

ZOO

(n.) Enclosed area where bizarre creatures from all over the world sit around eating, drinking and breeding. Not to be confused with Hong Kong's Discovery Bay or Shanghai's French Concession.

Other books by Larry Feign

方南理 **(Larry Feign)** is a writer, cartoonist, and animation director who has lived on the south China coast for over thirty years. His work has appeared in publications around the world, and he has produced and directed animation for Disney, Cartoon Network and others. His cartoons and animation have received several international awards. His mother still thinks he should have been a doctor.

www.larryfeign.com

Made in the USA
Middletown, DE
25 July 2020